I See

Collection

Alyssa Hawkins

BookLeaf
Publishing

Presentation by *BookLeaf Publishing*

Web: www.bookleafpub.com

E-mail: info@bookleafpub.com

ISBN: 9789357442824

First edition 2023

*I dedicate this to my mother, Jenlyn Hawkins,
but especially to my grandmother, Barbara
Peters, who continues to suffer from illiteracy.
Thank you both for your unconditional love and
support. I believe in myself because you
believed in me first.*

Assumptions are the Mother of All Mistakes

You can't even take one step in my shoes, forget
a mile
I carry it all on my own, I don't complain, I
simply smile

Power's not given to you, unfortunate but true
When I fully tap into mine, you won't even be
able to fathom the things I'll do

We all have two eyes, two ears and one mouth
for a reason
I don't talk much, but I'm privy to more than
meets the eye
For the quiet ones possess the knowledge that is
most seasoned
But go ahead, keep on assuming I'm the girl
who's too weird and shy

Assume and you'll make an ass out of me and u
But, say what…say nothing, and just keep on
doing you boo

I already foresee you realizing your grave
mistake
You'll wish you had another chance to treat me
right, a second take

Pretty Wings

BOOM! CRASH!
The sound of shattering glass
She covered her eyes, waiting for this stormy
scene to pass

Toxic cycles, broken promises—the rules of love
tangling around the bend
That first touch and glimpse gave her the
strength she needed to take flight
But only she held the power to put it all to an
eternal end

She finally decided to be seen and fought back
Faced forward and left him behind
Love was something she no longer wanted to
lack

She realized it was time for her to spread her
wings and fly
After all, the sky is the limit
A better life for her daughter, she did not want to
deny
Eventually, the right opportunity came on by
Her mindset had changed
And overwhelmed with happiness, she cried

I used to dwell on the past, but now I don't even bother
I want for nothing
For she was not only my mother, but also my father

Yeah, I could have hate for him in my heart
But mama told me not to from the start
After lifting herself up, she threw down the rope
I grew strong and resilient, and always found the scarce rays of hope

Growing up and looking at her face, oh so divine
I learned that in the darkness, we could still find a way to shine

Our chances of survival were damn near impossible, slim to none
Back then, looking at us
You couldn't even imagine what we'd become

Her resilience came with a certain kind of beauty
Getting us onto safe grounds became her sole purpose, her duty

Now it's my turn
To spread my wings and fly

I know it's far away ma
But I'll be back, don't you cry

I just wanna make you proud
And I'll always be your little girl
After all that you've done for me
Mom, my queen
You deserve the world

Small Talk

So classy, smart and easy on the eyes, you don't
even need foundation
You'd never know you were from the projects

You have eyes but you still can't see
They only exist on the foundation of plotted
class separation and racial bias that your kind
projects

Music to My Ears

Synchronized symphonies
Blissful ballads
Melodious music
Bounicing beats
Soulful songs

A spectrum of sounds simultaneously filling up
the room
The Black Flower, finally able to take permanent
root and bloom

Dropped harm for harmony to proliferate
humanity
Scrutiny switched out for oneness and unity
Generational, biased infections no longer
spreading like weeds
Finally able to cultivate our culture, all without
requests for immunity

After the night comes the refreshing morning
dew
We are well rested and finally at peace, all
achieved without using a piece

Now to restore what we once had, there's much more work we need to do

Ultimatum

Not a fan of chocolate but you're too vanilla for
me
Guess you never had that convo about the bird
and the bee

I succumbed, fell weak and let my guard down
for our flesh to become one
Just to not cum?

You love a woman who isn't afraid to speak her
mind
Until you stroke yourself right into a sexual bind

Turn away as you ask if I got mine
But the answer is heard in my voice
Women are meant to be savored like fine wine
Learn and take action or I'll replace you—no
other choice

Never Goes out of Style

A long revolution for an even longer owed
evolution
I don't believe in war, but declaring one may be
our only solution
For everything you touch turns to ruin and
causes pollution
Whatever happens, I better get my retribution
And if I should die I'd rather go out for a cause
and with a bang
You know the style—execution

A Handful Can't Handle

The handful who tried to dim your light
Couldn't stand to see Black Excellence shine so
bright

Whenever it gets tough to stick to the plan, think
about the near future and their faces full of
regret

Burn, baby burn! And let your presence be felt
to the point that they wish y'all never ever met

Blank Canvas

Imagine living in a country that began with
United
Where no one was kindly invited
And the minds, beliefs and interests of its
inhabitants were anything but aligned or
coincided

That's how life here was in the past, and like
many others, I wanted no parts
So I did not allow the "land of the free" to taint
me and take root into my soul or capture my
heart
You see, I envisioned a reset, a blank canvas—a
fresh start
To do this, the simplest solution was to just get
up and depart
But the minority unified and became the
majority, setting out to embody the change they
wished
to see, leaving behind a positive and permanent
mark

Today, this country is worlds away from how it
began, and I'll tell you how that came to be

Rather than communicating with weapons and war, we started communicating with wisdom and words
Now there is no more use for arms other than welcoming and open ones because there is no more violence, only peace

There are no more negative connotations or generalizations placed on you due to the color of your skin
Now everyone is measured by who they are inside and not out, not for what they are without but who they are within

And no one is treated differently based on their gender
We took on the roles of a molder and mender
We stopped silencing her and worked hard to restore and mend her

This is the new future we painted in our minds, our blank canvas
And to the future minds, we pass the baton and proudly hand this

[you and i]

you and i
Are like a rose covered in thorns

Sub rosa
With thorns as treacherous as the heart

The "Ladder" to Success

I hate being reminded of demographic disparity
Was Brown v. Board not passed almost seventy
years ago?
On behalf of my people, I inquire, as we need
more clarity

We all have a right to education and separate but
equal is illegal, they say
But when you pay us a two-minute visit in our
rooms, I know you see it all, clear as day

You may have ladders to climb to the top, but I
found mine while balancing on my inherited
stilts
Be wary when I finally do make it to where you
currently reside
As I intend on making sure that the heart of your
garden comes to an end and wilts

TBD

If what's on the mind is acknowledged before
the desires of the heart, why do they say to
follow the beat of your own drum?

Scanning each face in the room, no one else
seems to budge, but are they that cool, calm and
collected?

Invisible lines and unspoken rules contain the
voices that strain to uncover the depths of
reality, so does the truth really set you free?

Modified laws were enforced, but Roe v. Wade
revealed that statutes can be broken, and nothing
is set in stone, so are we really protected by the
seemingly impartial scales of justice?

You flip through all the channels, same sad story
with an ending we all know too well, so if it's
nothing new, why is it called the news?

An infinite amount of questions but not even a
handful of concrete answers and working
solutions. We ultimately all share the same

plight, but continue to cast it aside like a stone,
as if neglect prolongs the inevitable.

Red Summer

An all you can get killing spree for an entire
season
A target if you failed the brown paper bag test,
there was no other reason

But they didn't discriminate: babies, children,
aunts and mothers
They took so many innocent lives, and here we
are, taking for granted all our summers

A Woman's Worth

I know my value, it's you who needs to
recognize my worth
Out of the two of us, who possesses the ability to
give birth?

Not that my value solely relies on my womb
But it was a woman who nurtured you and
helped you grow and bloom

Love me, listen to me, hear me roar
And I'll be the wings and wind that make you
soar
I'll let you be the reason for my throat being
sore

But you're blocking your blessings
Thinking your net worth is more because you're
a man
But everything you boast that you do isn't even
half of what I can

Drown Them Out

A girl is drowning and a mother tells her son
don't look back
He points and shouts that she is dying, but you
see, the girl is black

Living proof that a child's heart starts out good
and pure
It's not a condition you're born with, so no law
can stop it or ever be the cure
Would the young boy grow up to break the
mindset cycle…too early to be so sure

You could feel the rumble of the approaching
train as a black man's lace is entangled on the
track
The boy, now a father with a stone cold heart,
tells his daughter to ignore the scene and turn
her back

You Fill the Space Between Night and Morning

Hopeful, everlasting, unwavering, jealous,
passionate, rarely ever easy but never
overbearing
That is the love I have brewed for you
My cup runneth over, drenched in both tears of
anger and elation
But I prefer to have too much emotion than too
little, especially when it comes to you
And a lack of care would only indicate that we
no longer do

I would give my life for you to have the best one
But I would die if your presence became absent
in mine

So I am begging you, down on my knees from
night until morning
Show me how to love you and I will embody all
of your needs and wants
I will wave my flag and surrender all that is me
to you
As losing you would cause me to relapse and I
would surely go into mourning

Picture Perfect

All that pressure you put on me to be perfect
Tell me, was it all worth it?

You loved me the best way you knew how
But the part I craved was nothing money could
buy, it was intangible
Only being a child, my cry for help to you was
not understandable

Thrown out into the world, so young and
damaged
I did everything I said I would, even in the face
of defeat, I still managed

Love is a verb so the word must come with
action
With a bit of distance came a healthier
interaction

At the end of it all, there's no one in the world
that I love most
So to better memories, let's make a toast

POTENTial

It exists within you
You just have to believe

Your mind can become the most toxic place to
visit
So make sure it's clean and beautiful

I See You

Unseen
Unfamiliar
Uninvited.
They may hear you
But I see you
A diamond under the pressure of fitting into
something so plain and round
Light travels faster than sound
So I will arrive first when the time comes to
    catch
        you
Even in the event that I am running late and you
should fall
Just read my words and absorb their black trails
of light
They will guide you back to your path and lift
you up to once again stand tall

Printed in the USA
CPSIA information can be obtained
at www.ICGtesting.com
LVHW011540050124
767941LV00091B/5158

9 789357 442824